Knit One Purl One
Add a Little Rhyme

By
Laurain Keys

Dedication

This book is dedicated to my family and friends who have badgered me for years to try to get some of my almost 200 poems out of the drawer and into print. My love and gratitude goes to them xx

Acknowledgement

I recently took part in a fundraising challenge and consequently joined a group of fellow knitters on social media. One morning I posted a little ditty that had popped into my head and was amazed to see 100+ reactions! The following day another ditty was posted and again received over 100 reactions together with comments telling me they were making the members smile and that I should try to put then into print
This is the result.

Contents

A Reason to Write

It has kindly been suggested
That I write a little book
For those who knit with needles
Or crochet with a hook.
It seems my little ditties
Are making people smile
So I thought about it daily
And pondered for a while
As I do my knitting
Thoughts run through my head
They're keeping me awake at night
As I lay in my bed
The final task is in your hands
This Little Ditty book
I hope that you enjoy it
When you have time to take a look.

Ode to a Knitter

Walking past a wool shop
We try and hide our eyes
But there's a magic magnet
That pulls us right inside.
We have a look at aran
And study double knit
Justify our reasons
For buying lots of it
We need to knit for reasons
Non-knitters won't understand
Like knitting for new babies
It's great to lend a hand
The wool is made from lambswool
And lambs are known to leap
That's why wool jumps in our baskets
Made for us to keep
Then homeward bound we carry
Our spoils from shopping spree
And if this ditty made you laugh
You're a yarn-a-holic like me!

The Knitting Lady

There was a lady who knitted
From morning until night
She knitted with many colours
The dark ones and the light
She knitted teddies for others
Cardis and jumpers too
When it came to knitting
There was nothing she couldn't do
Knitting was her passion
She did it every day
And even as a tiny tot
There were words that she could say
"K1 P1 then K2tog
C2B and C2F' and even "psso"
People thought she spoke in riddles
But little did they know
That her love of all things knitting
Would simply grow and grow
She knitted as a teenager
She knitted as a wife
The items that she knitted
Took over Her whole life!
This lady is an inspiration
And if I had my way
I too would stay at home
And do my knitting every day!

Colours

Lemon for a baby boy
Peach for a little girl
Here's some black and grey wool
Think I'll give socks a whirl
A jacket for John
A cardi for Sue
A bonnet for Charlie
That's what I'll do
I'll crochet up a blanket
And knit an HRH
Maybe even a bedtime gnome
I wonder how long they'll take?
My needles will be clacking
As my knitting grows and grows
The joy that sitting knitting brings
Only a knitter knows

Super Hero Knitter

I am a knitting Nanny
With needles all aflame
I stand for peace and harmony
Fighting bad feelings is my game.
There's a black dog called Depression
Sometimes raises up his head
I get my knitting needles
And lay my fears to bed.
When arthritis pain attacks my legs
And I can hardly move
I lose myself in patterns
Waiting for movement to improve
When the family all go out
And leave me alone at night
I knit and purl and purl and knit
To my heart's delight.
With my trusty knitting needles
I never feel forlorn
Choose another ball of wool
And creativity is born
A cardi for my little niece
A jumper for a nephew
A ballerina and a rhino

I've knitted Star Wars figures too
I've knitted many many things
And kept my problems away
That's why I'm a Super Hero
And why I knit every day every day

Not just for the Ladies

Tom Daly is an athlete
With medals to his name
But when he's not competing
Knitting is his game.
Ewan McGregor is an actor
Who has an award or two
And when he is relaxing
Knitting is what he'll do
Ryan Gosling, Russel Crowe
To name but a few
Are gentlemen who like to knit
A homemade item or two.
Some people think that Knitting
Is not a thing for men
Just Google the men knitters
And make them think again
So when your hubby questions
Your stash of yarn and pins
Just turn around and mention
That you bought some spare for him

Essential Shopping

Saturday is shopping day
though it's not very cool
I need to make a shopping list
Tea, butter, sugar, WOOL
I need to get a toilet roll
Some cereal and crisps
WOW! that WOOL is a bargain
I really can't resist!
I could have shopped in Tesco
Or popped into Waitrose
But Aldi's have the bargain WOOL
As every knitter knows
I'll tell hubby that I'm saving
Watching pennies more and more
But in truth I am hoarding WOOL
and accessories galore!!

The Knitting Challenge

Through the month of March
I Knitted, I purled,
I slipped one, knitted 2 together
And passed the slip over
Cast on, cast off
It's time for another
Today I think I need a break
So with a special friend
A lunch I will take
I will give her a cardi
I made for her granddaughter
Tomorrow I will knit
And do as I oughta (sorry)
But just for today
My needles will rest
My head will then clear
And I can give my best
To the bedtime gnome
And the other small bits
To use up some wool
With lots of new knits.

Blanket for Sue

I made a little blanket
For my dolly Sue
Mummy had no time for it
So showed me what to do.
She gave me wool and needles
With a loop quite near the end
needle in, wrap the wool
Pull it through and repeat again.
Well I tried to follow what she said I
But somehow made a hole
I'm sure that it won't matter
I just need more control.
The needles are too big for me
They move around the place
If I'm not very careful
Then they poke me in the face.
Anyway I kept knitting
And did my very best
Dropped some stitches as I went
So I just knitted the rest.

Mummy made me 40 stitches
On row, 4 there were fifty three
I don't know how I added more
Clever little me!
Sue loves the finished blanket
As I push her in her pram
And all the family tell me
What a clever girl I am.
I made a dolly blanket
To cover Sue's hands and feet
A dropped stitch here a knot right there
Dont care that it's not neat.
Next week I'll make a cardigan
But use some smaller "sticks
They might make knitting better
Because I'm only six.

New Hobby

Knit one purl one
Drop a stitch or two
I've started a new hobby
But I haven't got a clue
I blame it on a friend of mine
Who bought me a little kit?
"Stop playing computer games all day
And teach yourself to knit"
Well I tore the packet open
And I settled down with glee
But all of the instructions
Were just gobblygook to me?
I studied the book so carefully
My face it wore a frown
K1? P1? psso?
I threw the damn book down
I thought I'd go online again
And check out videos
To show exactly what to do
Must be someone who knows!

Thankfully, I found one
And finally I know
Just what the little squiggles mean
And I can have a go.
The wool was multi coloured
The needles wooden sticks
I persevered and conquered
All of the fiddly bits
Now I stay off the computer
And I really have to say
Learning how to knit my friend
Has really made my day.
I watch my knitting growing
And I create with pride
Wherever I go wandering
My knitting is by my side.
So if you're feeling restless
And bored with life's routine
Buy yourself a little kit
And become a knitting queen.

For my Grandson

A brand new ball of knitting yarn
Needles at the ready
These 100g balls of chestnut brown
Will soon become a Teddy.
I'll knit it up with love
And give to a little boy
Then watch him as he hugs it
And his face lights up with joy
He's looked at all my patterns
And made a heartfelt plea
"Nanny could you possibly
Make one of these for me?"
Knitting is a pleasure
When done for family
The joy on all their faces
Is worth it all for me

My Mother

Memories of my mother
With needles in her hands
She always wove some magic
With her woolen strands
I am one of five children
And she knitted for us all
We often held our hands out
As she wound from skein to ball
The boys had matching jumpers
Cardigans for us girls
Lovingly created
With the use of knits and purls
I remember in the 60s
She knitted me a dress
With rows of blue and yellow
I loved it I confess
When I was in my pre-teens
Mum showed me how to knit
For a while I struggled
Could not get on with it

When I became an adult
And my first born child was due
Mum knitted lots of baby clothes
In lemon, white and blue.
Patiently she showed me
The things that I must do
To become a decent knitter
And kit out my children too
Now mum's no longer with us
But I'm sure that she will know
How her knitwear inspired me
And made my love for knitting grow

Learning to Crochet

I bought myself some white wool
And a nifty little hook
Watched some clips on YouTube
And bought a "How to" book
I made myself a coffee
And sat down in my chair
Determined I would crochet
Something that I could wear
I made a chain of stitches
It was going very well
But how to do the next step
I really couldn't tell
It seemed I had to double back
On chains that I'd just done
I was beginning to feel that
Crochet really wasn't fun.
I looked again at the pattern
"Miss 3 chain" it said
But I have only made one chain
Growled the voices in my head.

When I buy a necklace
The bits are all called a link
But the little bits I crochet
Are all called chains I think.
I worked on my creation
Many times, I had to frog
But in the end I realized
I'd made a nice dish cloth!
That was many years ago
And now I can crochet
But for ease and stress free work
Give me knitting any day

If I won the Lottery

If I won the lottery
No question what I'd do
I'd open up a wool shop
For crafters just like you.
I'd have yarn a plenty
In every colour hue
Stock needles, hooks and more
Have a pattern swap stop too.
In the corner would be a table
With chairs all draped in blue
Where we could sit and natter
And help those without a clue.
I'd store some yarn on lay-away
As wool shops used to do
As long as it was purchased
Within a month or two.
I'd set up crafting classes
For adults and children too
Men would also be welcome
To learn a new skill too
My dream is just a fantasy
I doubt it will come true
But my win on the lottery
Is extremely overdue

W-I-P

They call it work in progress
The knitting that we leave
Sometimes it's a complete side
Sometimes it's just a sleeve.
People say it's wasting
The wool that we all keep
Not to finish knitting
Until the garment is, complete
May I please explain to you?
The reason why we stop
It's usually because we find
New wool in a shop
This new wool seems to call to us
"Oh buy me and you'll see
The new and wonderful designs
You can create with me"
And so we buy this new wool
And find a pattern that will suit
Then carry home our treasure
And go off on a new route
Once we have finished knitting

We happily return to
The work we left in progress
With energy renewed
So please don't moan about
Our knitting W-I-P
Sometimes a new task rejuvenates
Our creativity.

What Made Me Write?

One day when I was feeling bored
I wrote a little rhyme
All about my knitting
With which I passed my time.
I posted it on Facebook
To a group that shares its knits
The next day I was astounded
To find it was a hit.
Some people asked me if I could
Post a poem every day
Apparently, it made them smile
And some went on to say
"You should try and publish
Your poems are quite good"
This was something that I'd thought of
But I didn't think I could
The group was so supportive
And so many of them said
"You have to take a leap of faith
You have to go ahead"
And so I trawled the internet

To see what I had to do
Then sat down at my laptop
To write a poem or two
I hope that what you are reading
Is good enough for you
And that if you're feeling brave enough
You'll write some poems too.

During Lockdown

The little knitting industries
We're going out of fashion
Buying cheap commodities
Became a high street passion
Knitwear then was mass-produced
And hit the local store
Similar designs and styles
Were what the people wore
Then came the pandemic
To our homes we were confined
Boredom made us look again
At how to pass our time
We pulled out knitting needles
That had been packed away
And rediscovered balls of yarn
We had bought some previous day
Knitting maintained our sanity
The hobby was revived
As we endured the lockdowns
It helped us to survive

Yarn was ordered online
And delivered to out door
To be knitted into cardigans
Jumper's toys and more
Now the situation has improved
And we are free to roam
But many people still enjoy
Knitting while at home
I hope these newfound talents
Quickly become a trend
And good old fashioned knitting
Becomes popular again.

The Bargain

Had a ball of knitting yarn
That got me all excited
I really was delighted
Knowing what I would knit with them
Had me all excited
The weight was double knitting
The colours blew my mind
I searched through knitting patterns
To see what I could find
I pulled out all my pattern files
And finally found a box
I saw the sheet I was looking for
"How to make long socks"
Did you think I'd make a jumper?
Or a smart hat for my head?
Sorry to disappoint you but
My feet get cold in bed!
The balls of wool were perfect
And I noted happily
The wool was such a bargain!
Reduced to 50p!

Sewing In

I've made a beautiful jumper
I think it's called Fair isle
I started it in January
It's taken me awhile
At times, I became tempted
To rip the whole thing out
When all the wool got tangled
I admit it made me shout
It took four weeks to finish
Nearly drove me round the bends
Especially when I realised
Each colour had two ends!
Now knitting is my forte
I'm excited to begin
The only part I really hate
Is sewing the ends in.
I sit with darning needle
And try to thread the eye
I try and try so many times
It almost makes me cry
But when the jumpers finished
And the sewing is all done
I always look for patterns
And start another one

Distraction

I settled down to watch TV
On a Saturday afternoon
It was a snooker championship
And it was quiet in the room
The competition was quite serious
My eyes were so transfixed
But then I heard the dreaded noise
CLICK CLICK CLICK CLICK CLICK
My eyes slowly swiveled
To my wife sat next to me
With her needles clicking
And her knitting on her knee
A cheer went up upon the screen
The black ball had been potted
My wife's moaning had distracted me
When her wool had become knotted
I'd missed the final winning shot
I really was quite mad
But my wife just sat there counting
All the stitches that she had.

She caught me staring at her
And flashed a smile at me
"Oh great the match has finished
Would you like a cup of tea?"
She'd been in the world of knitters
Where she often seems to go
But the little things distract me
And she doesn't even know!
Clicking of the needles
Counting regularly
Keep flicking over patterns
That are resting on her knee
It's not done on purpose
She doesn't realise
But all these little movements
Always draw my eyes
Next time I want to concentrate
On the sports events I love
I think I'll leave her knitting
And watch it in the pub!

Casting off

My little book of knitting odes
Is finally complete
The contents have been typed out
And it's all bound up so neat
This book has been a challenge
Something I never thought I'd do
Class of 22 Crafters
It's all because of you.
Like many fellow knitters
When our knitting is all done
It's time for me to cast off
Thank you - it's been fun

Printed in Great Britain
by Amazon